WOW®
2001
SONGBOOK

THE YEAR'S 30 TOP CONTEMPORARY CHRISTIAN ARTISTS AND HITS

WoW Hits 2001 recorded on Sparrow cassette #724385177941, CD #724385177927

Edited by

BRYCE INMAN & KEN BARKER

Transcribed by

Bryce Inman, Bill Wolaver,
Danny Zaloudik, Brent Roberts,
Ken Barker and Lee Marcum

WORD MUSIC®

WOW 2001

CONTENTS

Dive

Recorded by Steven Curtis Chapman

Words and Music by
STEVEN CURTIS CHAPMAN

1. The long a-wait-ed rains have fall-en hard up-on the thirst-y ground;
2. There is a su-per-nat-'ral pow-er in the might-y riv-er's flow.

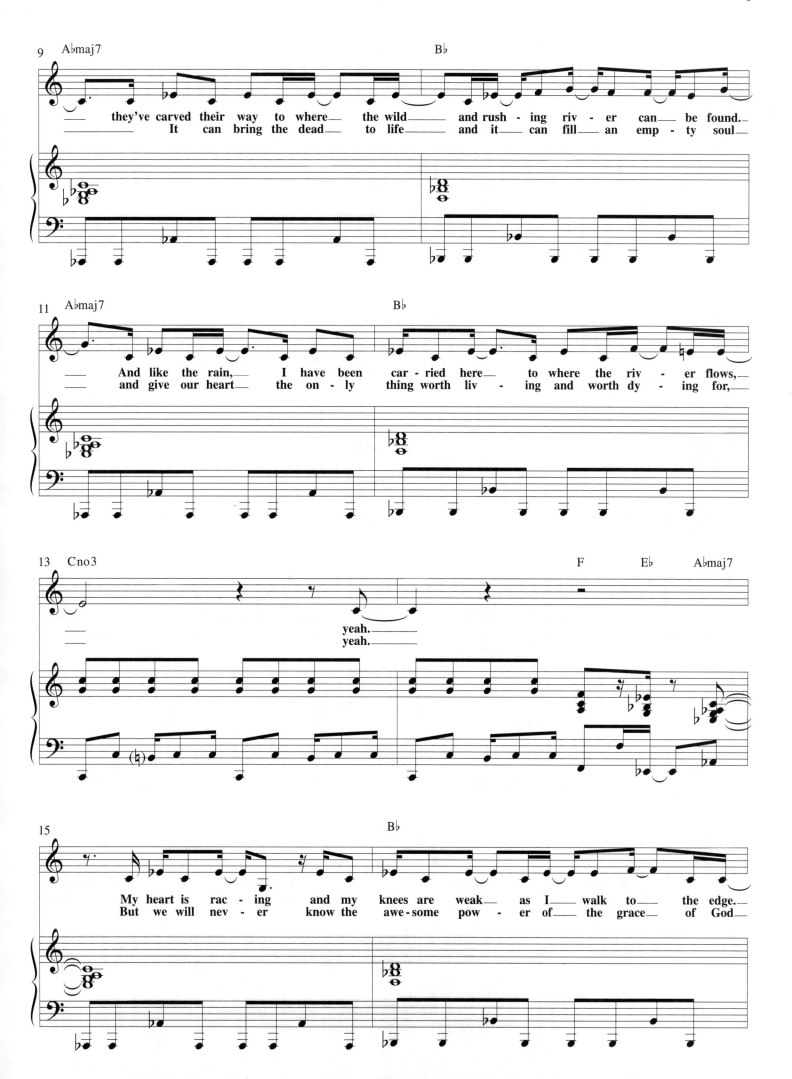

Live for You

Recorded by Rachael Lampa

Words and Music by
CHRIS EATON
and CHRIS RODRIGUEZ

Latin pop feel ♩ = 88

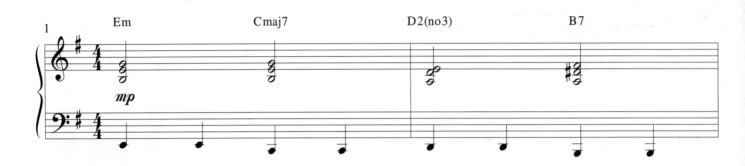

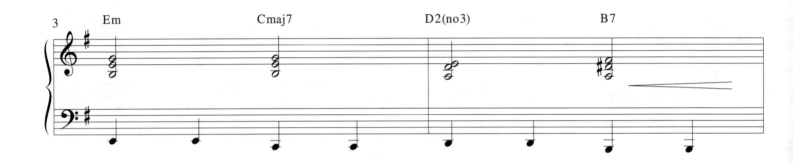

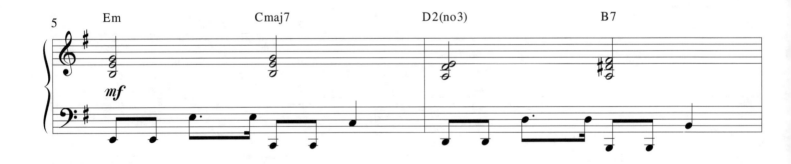

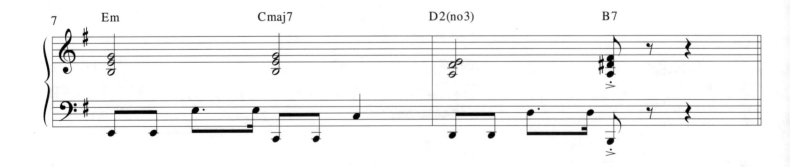

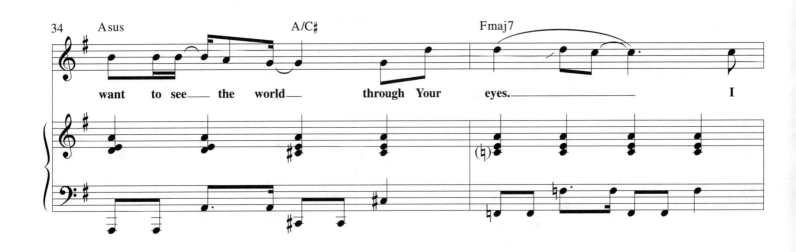

want to see the world through Your eyes. I

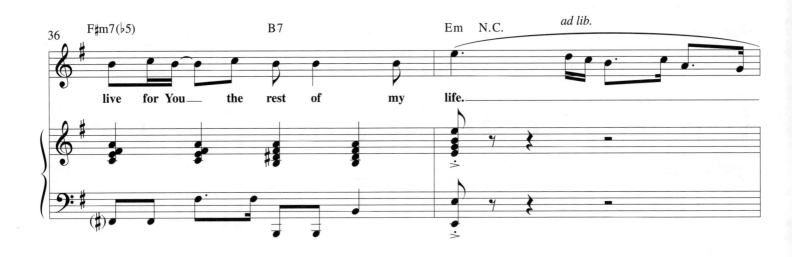

live for You the rest of my life.

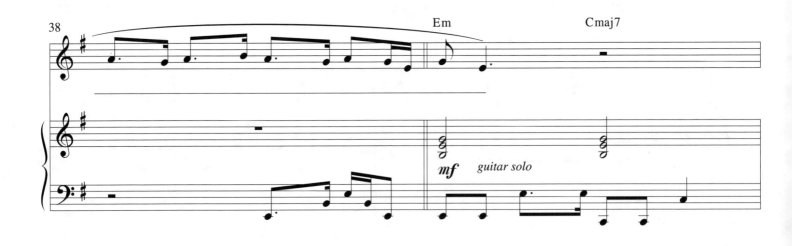

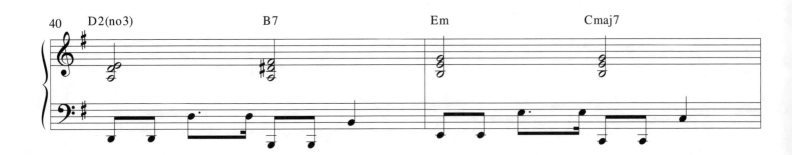

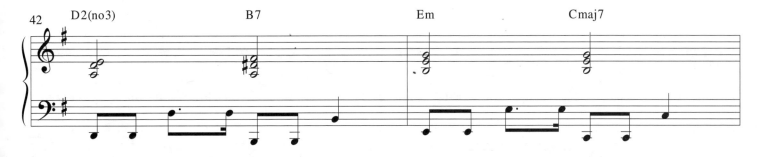

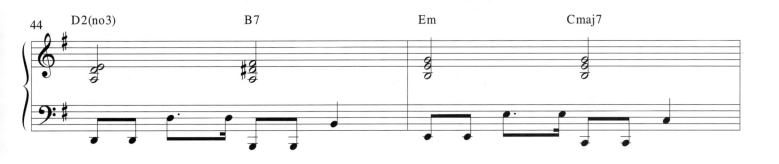

I live for You,— I live— for You,—
(life.)

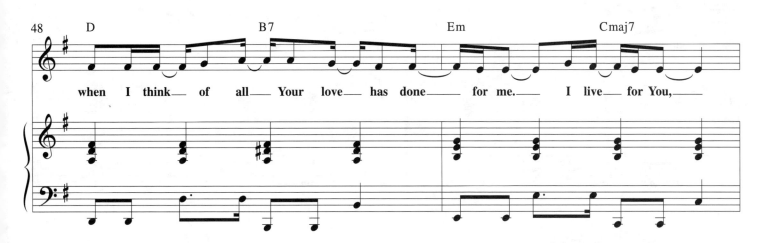

when I think— of all— Your love— has done— for me.— I live— for You,—

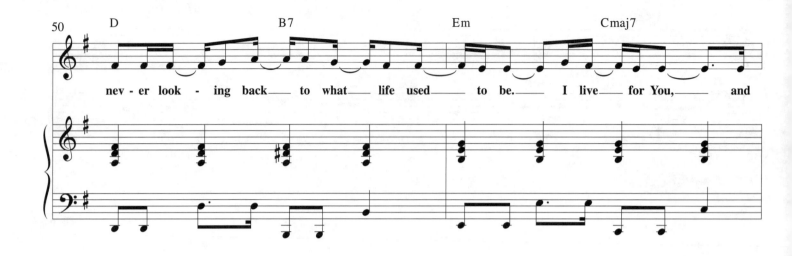

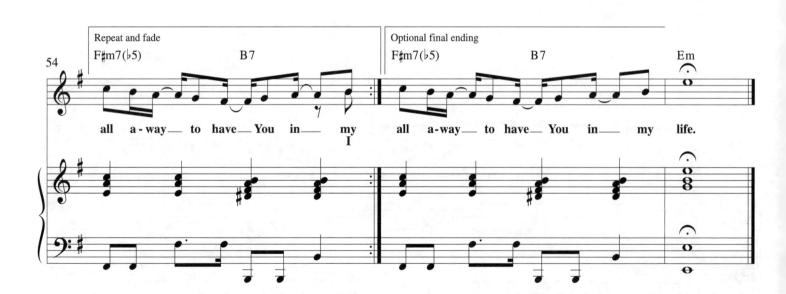

Written on My Heart

Recorded by Plus One

Words and Music by
ERIC FOSTER WHITE and
STEPHANIE LEWIS

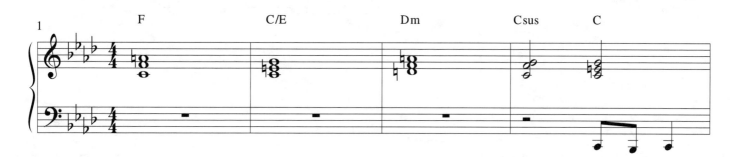

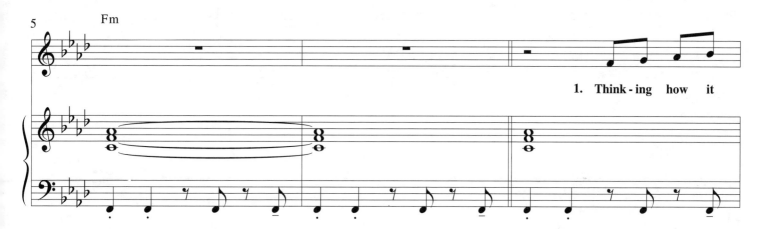

"Inspired by and in memory of Cassie Bernall. I look forward to meeting you on the other side."

This Is Your Time

Recorded by Michael W. Smith

**Words and Music by
MICHAEL W. SMITH
and WES KING**

Alabaster Box

Recorded by CeCe Winans

**Words and Music by
JANICE SJOSTRAN**

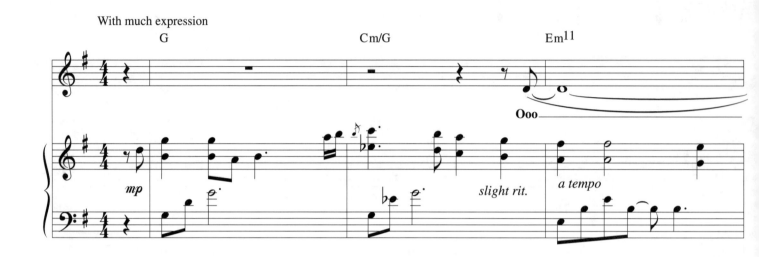

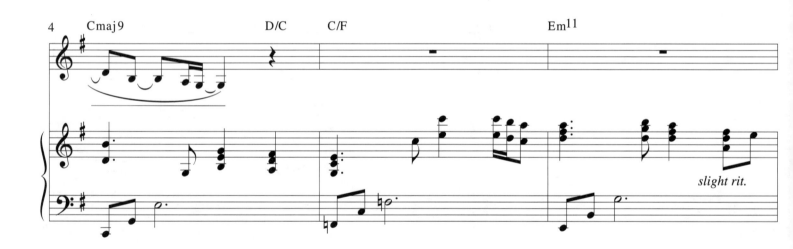

Gather at the River (Remix)

Recorded by Point of Grace

Words and Music by
JOEL LINDSEY
and REGIE HAMM

48

Always Have, Always Will

Recorded by Avalon

**Words and Music by
NICK GONZALES, GRANT CUNNINGHAM
and TOBY McKEEHAN**

Moderately ♩ = 93

Crystal Clear

Recorded by Jaci Velasquez

Words and Music by
MATT STANFIELD
and TIFFANY ARBUCKLE

2nd time to CODA ⊕

Every Season

Recorded by Nichole Nordeman

Words and Music by
NICHOLE NORDEMAN

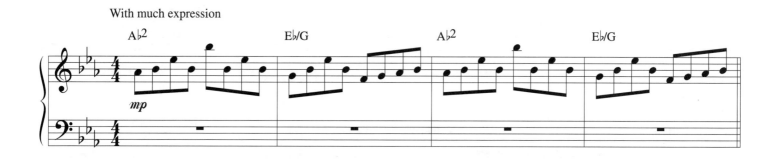

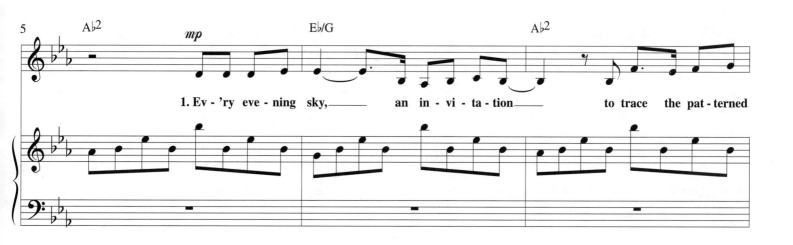

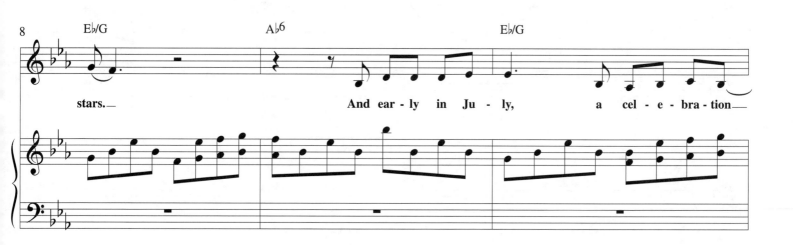

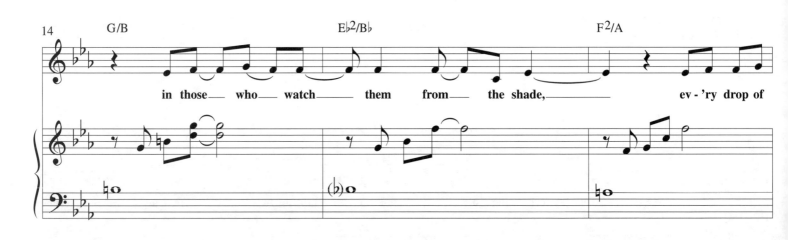

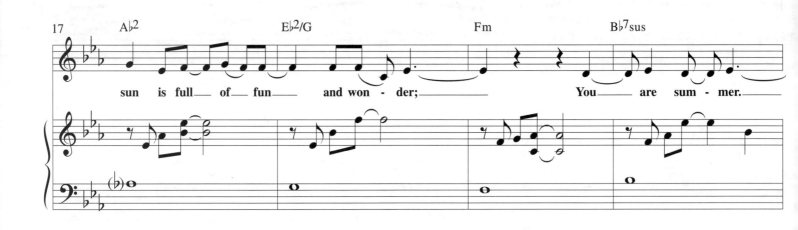

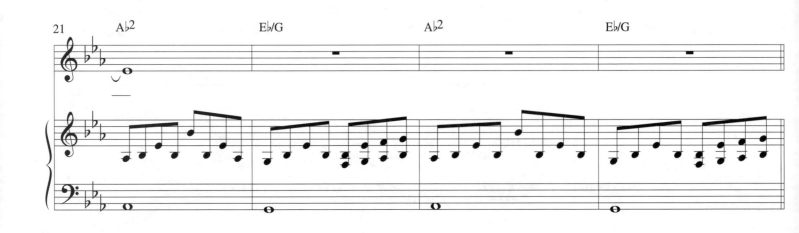

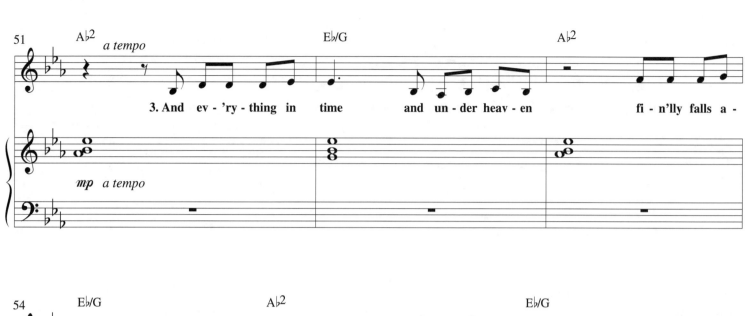

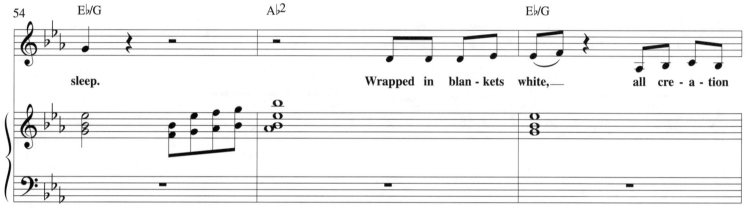

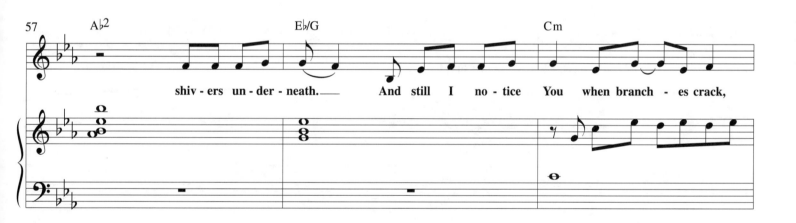

I Am the Way

Recorded by Mark Schultz

Words and Music by
MARK SCHULTZ

Pop feel ♩ = 112

got a **se** - **cret** no — one **knows** — locked a - way — where no — one **goes,** —
2. So you **want** a **brand** new **start** — ask - in' **Me** — in - to — your **heart,** —

1. You've

Free

Recorded by Ginny Owens

Words and Music by
GINNY OWENS

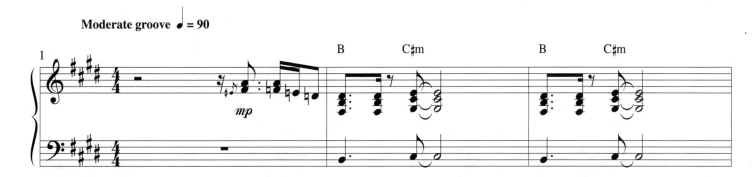

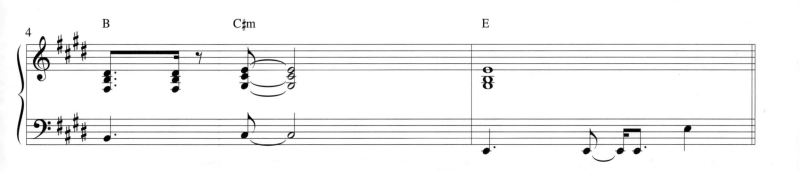

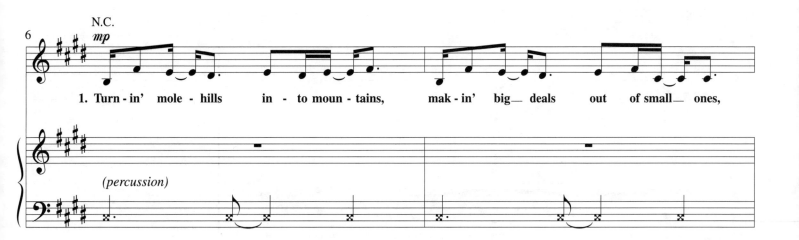

1. Turn - in' mole - hills in - to moun - tains, mak - in' big— deals out of small— ones,

More Than You'll Ever Know

Recorded by Watermark

Words and Music by
NATHAN and CHRISTY NOCKELS

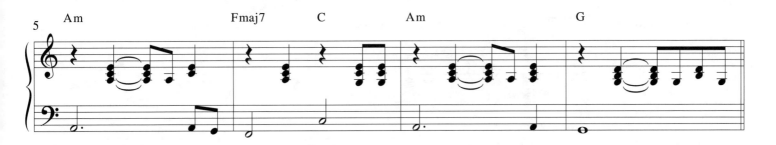

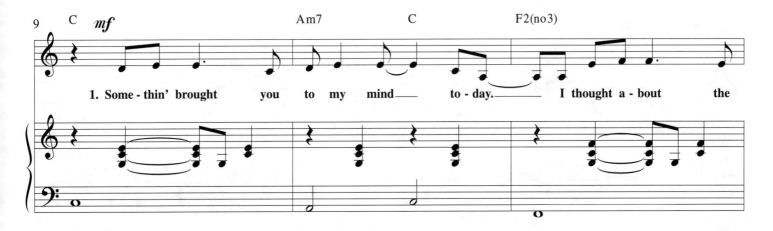

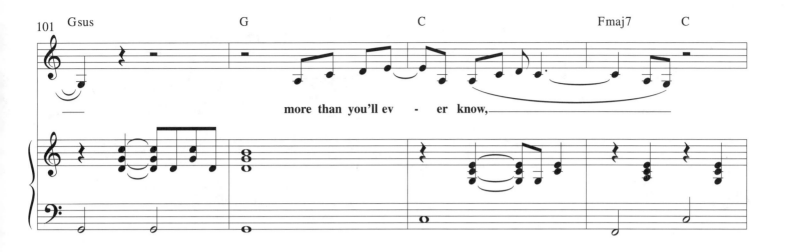

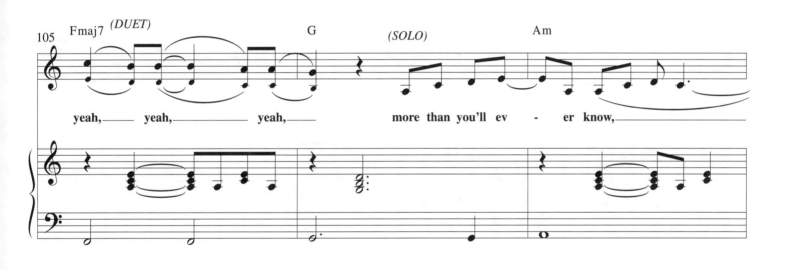

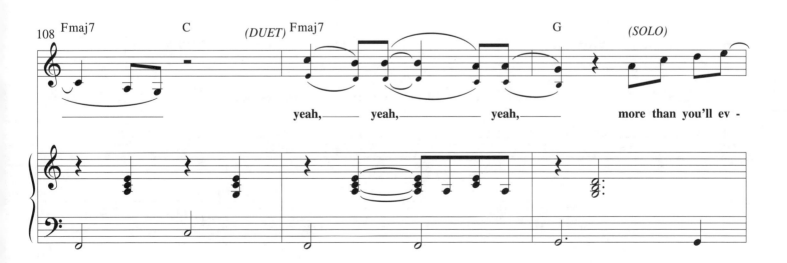

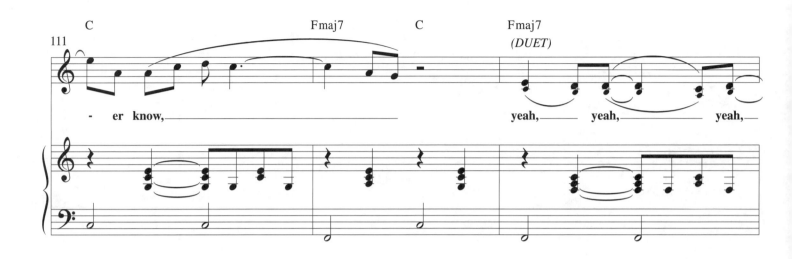

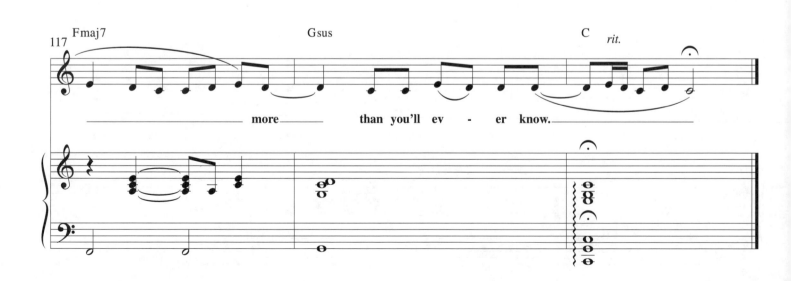

When I Praise

Recorded by FFH

Words and Music by
JEROMY DEIBLER

This Good Day

Recorded by Fernando Ortega

**Words and Music by
FERNANDO ORTEGA and
JOHN ANDREW SCHREINER**

I lift___ my___ voice___ to sing a song___ of praise___

___ on this___ good day.___

Redeemer

Recorded by Nicole C. Mullen

**Words and Music by
NICOLE COLEMAN-MULLEN**

Lord, I Come Before You

Recorded by Salvador

**Words and Music by
ART GONZALES, NICK GONZALES
and MATTHEW WEST**

Set Your Eyes to Zion

Recorded by P.O.D.

**Words and Music by
NOAH BERNANDO, PAUL SANDOVAL,
MARK DANIELS and MARCOS CURIEL**

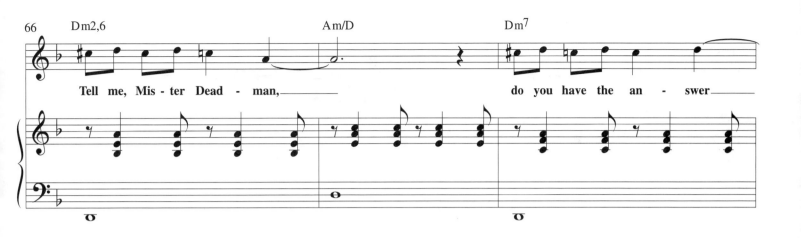

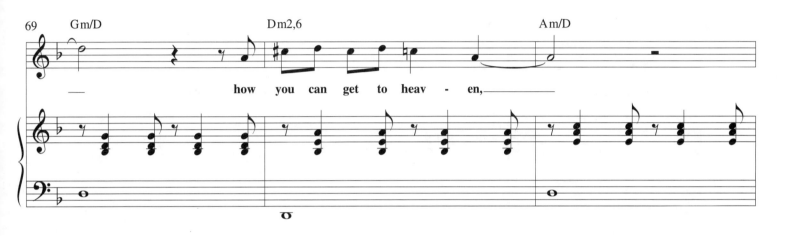

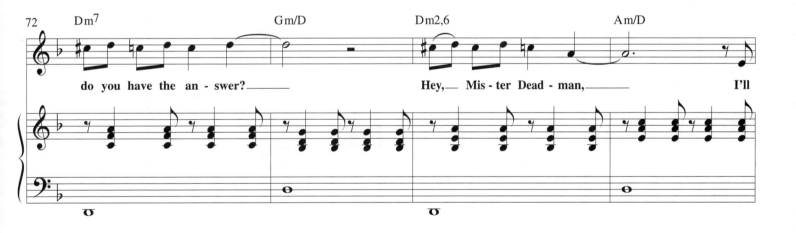

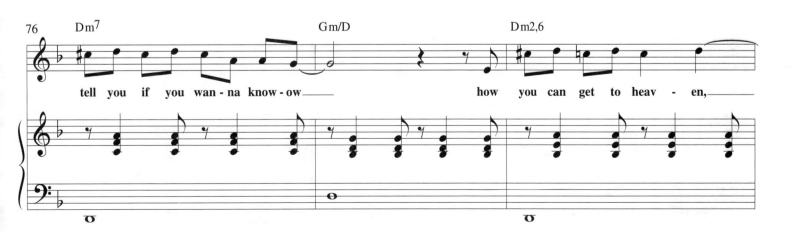

Shackles (Praise You)

Recorded by Mary, Mary

Words and Music by
WARRYN CAMPBELL, ERICA ATKINS
and **TRECINA ATKINS**

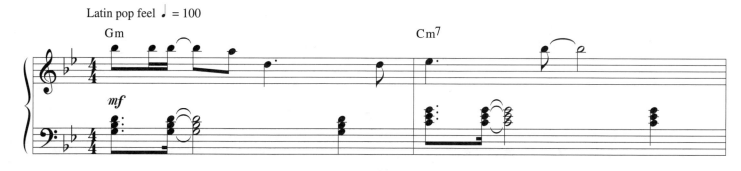

King of Glory

Recorded by Third Day

MAC POWELL   **THIRD DAY**

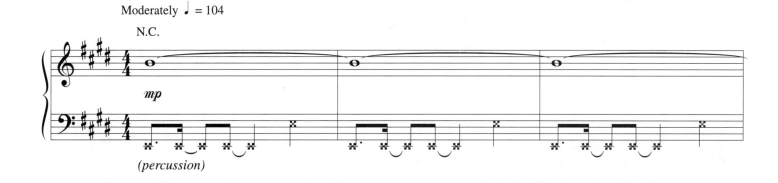

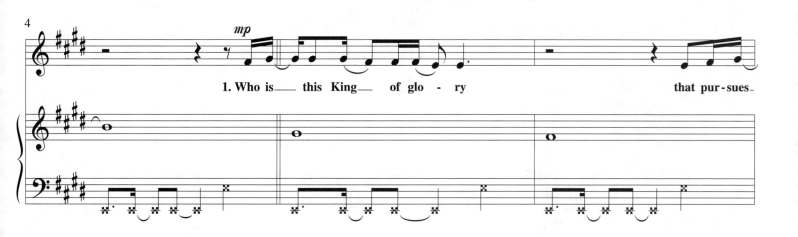

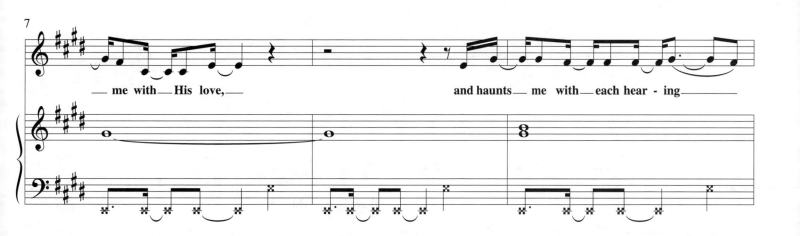

(percussion figure continues)

Beautiful Sound

Recorded by Newsboys

**Words and Music by
PETER FURLER and
PHIL JOEL**

In four, with a beat ♩ = 112

1. Turn the page,— can't turn the light— out,— ev - 'ry

word, ev - 'ry line car - ries to— my— soul; dark

Lyrics: I won't stop___ now that I'm free,___ I'll be chas-in' You___ like You chase me.

Into You

Recorded by Jennifer Knapp

Words and Music by
JENNIFER KNAPP

Red Letters

Recorded by DC Talk

**Words and Music by
TOBY McKEEHAN, MICHAEL TAIT, KEVIN MAX
MARK HEIMERMANN and CHRIS HARRIS**

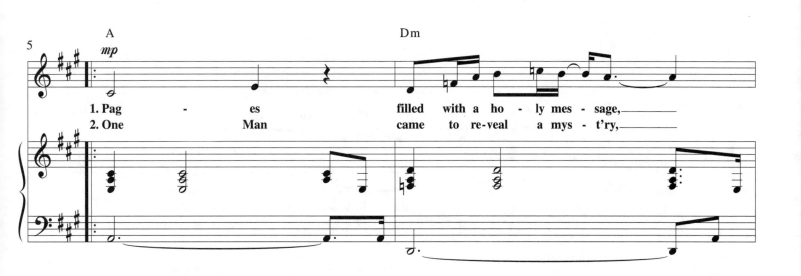

1. Pag - es filled with a ho - ly mes - sage,_____
2. One Man came to re - veal a mys - t'ry,_____

sealed with a kiss from heav - en, on a scroll,___ long a - go,___
chang - ing the course of his - t'ry. Made the claim___ He was God,___

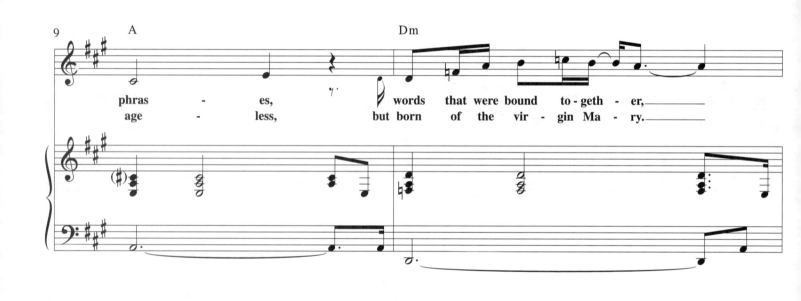

phras - es, words that were bound to - geth - er,___
age - less, but born of the vir - gin Ma - ry.___

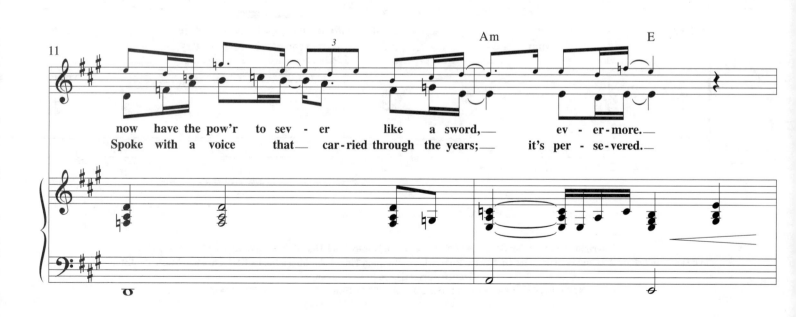

now have the pow'r to sev - er like a sword,___ ev - er-more.___
Spoke with a voice that___ car-ried through the years;___ it's per - se-vered.___

Unforgetful You

Recorded by Jars of Clay

Words and Music by
DAN HASELTINE, MATT ODMARK,
STEPHEN MASON and CHARLIE LOWELL

The Only One

Recorded by Caedmon's Call

**Words and Music by
AARON TATE**

Moderate rock feel ♩ = 105

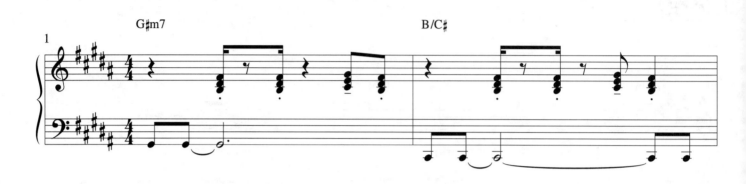

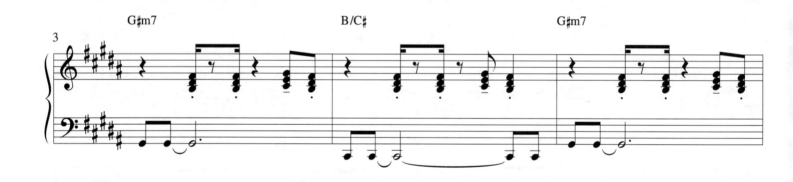

Reborn

Recorded by Rebecca St. James.

**Words and Music by
REBECCA ST. JAMES and
MATT BRONLEEWE**

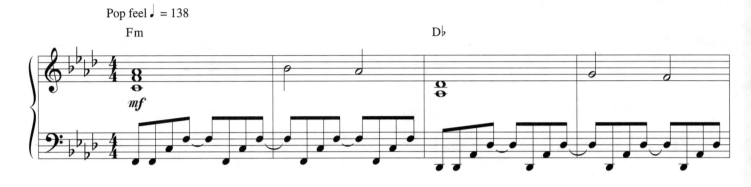

If you see a change in me,—— don't won-der; there's

God, You Are My God

Recorded by Delirious

**Words and Music by
STUART GARRARD**

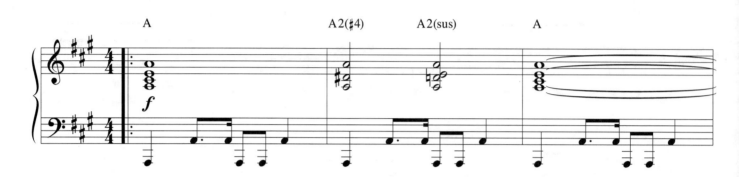

Follow Your Dreams

Recorded by Raze

Words and Music by
MICHAEL-ANTHONY TAYLOR
and TOMMY SIMMS

Don't Look at Me

Recorded by Stacie Orrico

Words and Music by
MARK HEIMERMANN and
STACIE ORRICO

God of Wonders

Recorded by Mac Powell (Third Day) and
Cliff and Danielle Young (Caedmon's Call)

Words and Music by
MARC BYRD and
STEVE HINDALONG

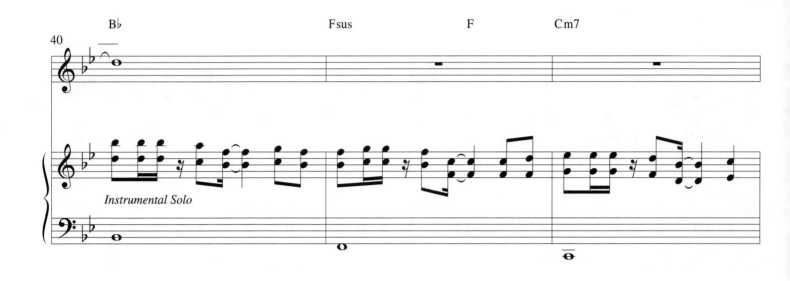

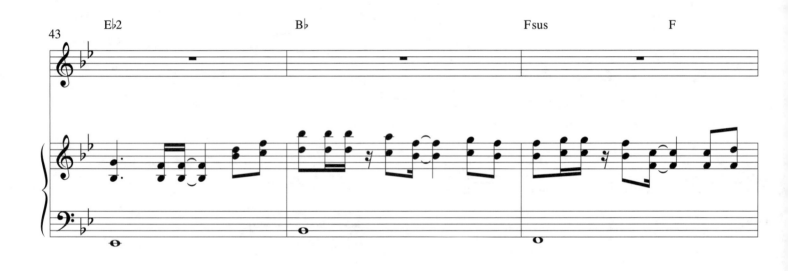

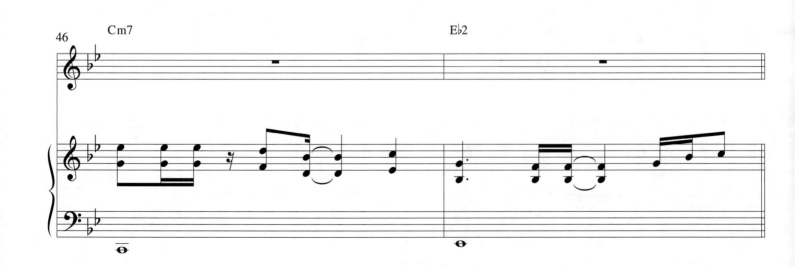

God of won - ders be - yond our gal - ax - y, You are

ho - ly,____ ho - ly.____

Pre - cious Lord,____ re - veal____ Your heart____ to me, Fath - er

ho - ly,____ ho - ly,____ the

America

Recorded by Passion: One Day

Words and Music by
CHRIS TOMLIN, J.D. WALT
and JACK PARKER

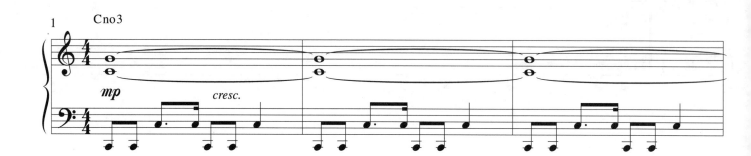

It's blow - ing through,___ it's com - ing to___ A - mer - i - ca___ a - gain.

com-ing to___ A-mer - i - ca.___   Can you feel the fi - re?

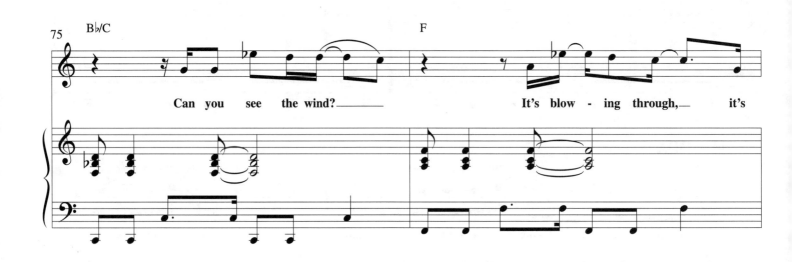

Can you see the wind?___   It's blow - ing through,___ it's

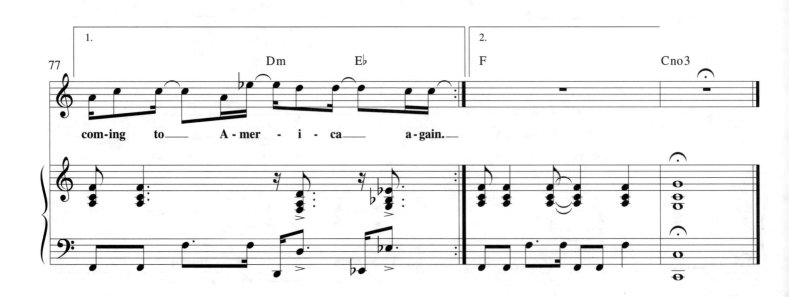

com-ing to___ A-mer - i - ca___ a - gain.___

Hands and Feet

Recorded by Audio Adrenaline

**Words and Music by
MARK STUART, BOB HERDMAN, WILL McGINNISS,
TYLER BURKUM and CHARLIE PEACOCK**

Whitehorse

Recorded by Earthsuit

**Words and Music by
PAUL MEANY, ADAM LaCLAVE
and STEVE SOLOMON**

Where I Wanna Be

Recorded by V-enna

**Words and Music by
MARK PENNELLS
and ZARC PORTER**

Rock drive ♩ = 116

1. I wan-na be the way You are.— Don't wan-na be the one to
2. I wan-na love the way You love.— The love that I can give is

OTHER ARTIST RELATED
FOLIOS

The following songs are also available in the artist folios listed:

Always Have, Always Will (AVALON)
Available through Chordant in the songbook "In a Different Light" —
Hal Leonard (HL00306295)

America (PASSION: ONE DAY LIVE)
Available through Chordant in the songbook
"Worship Together Songbook 3.0" —
Worshiptogether.com (SB1256)

Crystal Clear (JACI VELASQUEZ)
Available in the songbook "Crystal Clear" —
Word Music (080689378387)

Dive (STEVEN CURTIS CHAPMAN)
Available through Chordant in the songbook "Speechless" —
Hal Leonard (HL00306316)

Every Season (NICHOLE NORDEMAN)
Available through Chordant in the songbook "This Mystery" —
Hal Leonard (HL00306366)

Gather at the River (Remix)
(POINT OF GRACE)
Available in the songbook "Rarities and Remixes" —
Word Music (080689365287)

God of Wonders (CITY ON A HILL)
Available in the songbook "City on a Hill" —
Brentwood-Benson Music Publishing (4575703877)

God, You Are My God (DELIRIOUS)
Available through Chordant in the songbook "Glo" —
Hal Leonard (HL00306386)

Hands and Feet (AUDIO ADRENALINE)
Available through Chordant in the songbook
"The Best of Audio Adrenaline"
Hal Leonard (HL00690418)

I Am the Way (MARK SCHULTZ)
Available in the songbook "Mark Schultz"
Word Music (080689376283)

Into You (JENNIFER KNAPP)
Available through Chordant in the songbook "Lay It Down" —
Hal Leonard (HL00306358)

King of Glory (THIRD DAY)
Available in the songbook "Offerings" —
Brentwood-Benson Music Publishing (4575703847)

Live for You (RACHAEL LAMPA)
Available in the songbook "Live for You" —
Word Music (080689377280)

More Than You'll Ever Know
(WATERMARK)
Available in the songbook "The Watermark Songbook" —
Word Music (080689374289)

Red Letters (DC TALK)
Available through Chordant in the songbook "Supernatural" —
Hal Leonard (HL00690333)

This Good Day (FERNANDO ORTEGA)
Available in the songbook "Home" —
Word Music (080689359286)

This Is Your Time (MICHAEL W. SMITH)
Available in the songbook "This Is Your Time" —
Hal Leonard (HL00306384)

Unforgetful You (JARS OF CLAY)
Available in the songbook "If I Left the Zoo" —
Brentwood-Benson Music Publishing (4575702507)

When I Praise (FFH)
Available in the songbook "Found a Place" —
Brentwood-Benson Music Publishing (4575703137)

RECORDINGS

CURRENTLY AVAILABLE FROM THE WOW SERIES

WOW 1996
Sparrow Records
(CD SPD1516;
Cassette SPC1516)

WOW 1997
Sparrow Records
(CD SPD1562;
Cassette SPC1562)

WOW 1998
Sparrow Records
(CD SPD1629;
Cassette SPC1629)

WOW 1999
Sparrow Records
(CD SPD1686;
Cassette SPC1686)

WOW 2000
Sparrow Records
(CD SPD1703;
Cassette SPC1703)

WOW 2001
Sparrow Records
(CD 724385177927;
Cassette 724385177941)

WOW the 90s
Word Entertainment
(CD 080688580728;
Cassette 080688580742)

WOW Gold
Provident Music Group
(CD 8306105332;
Cassette 8306105334)

WOW Worship
(Blue)
Integrity Music
(CD 000768158326;
Cassette 000768158340)

WOW Worship
(Orange)
Integrity Music
(CD 000768172322;
Cassette 000768172346)

WOW Gospel 1998
Verity Records
(CD 1241431092;
Cassette 1241431094)

WOW Gospel 1999
Verity Records
(CD 1241431252;
Cassette 1241432594)

WOW Gospel 2000
Verity Records
(CD 1241431492;
Cassette 1241431494)